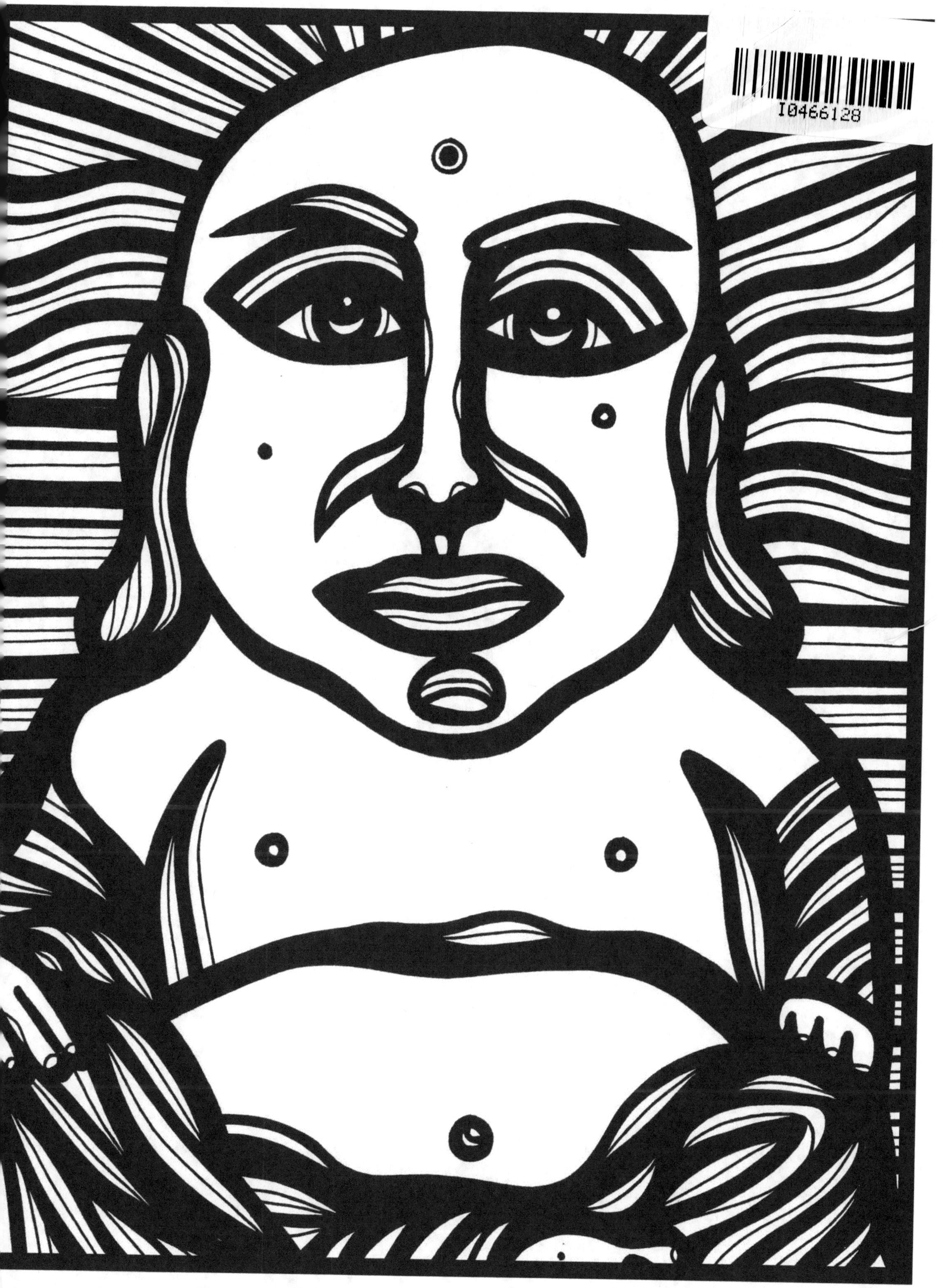

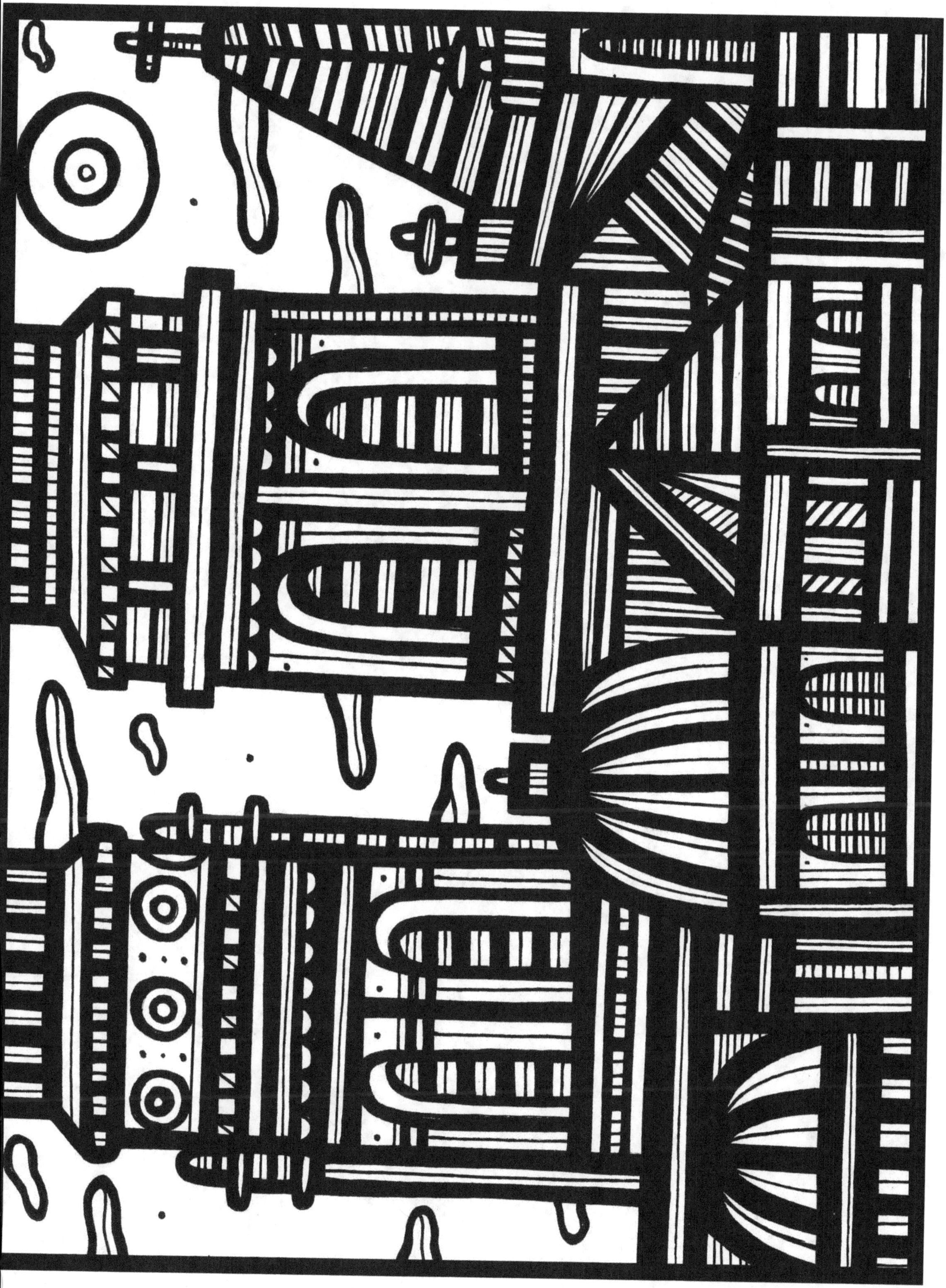

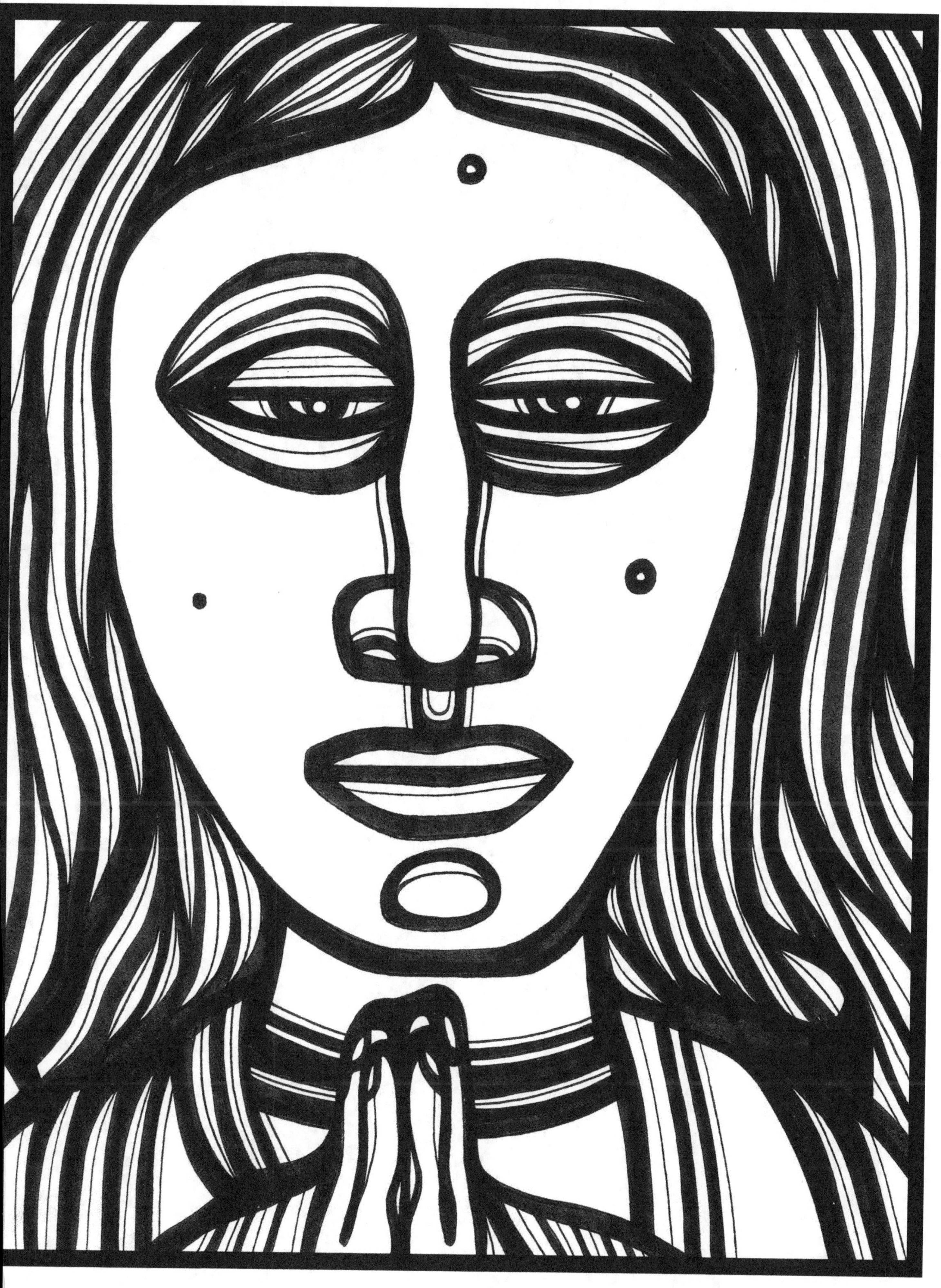

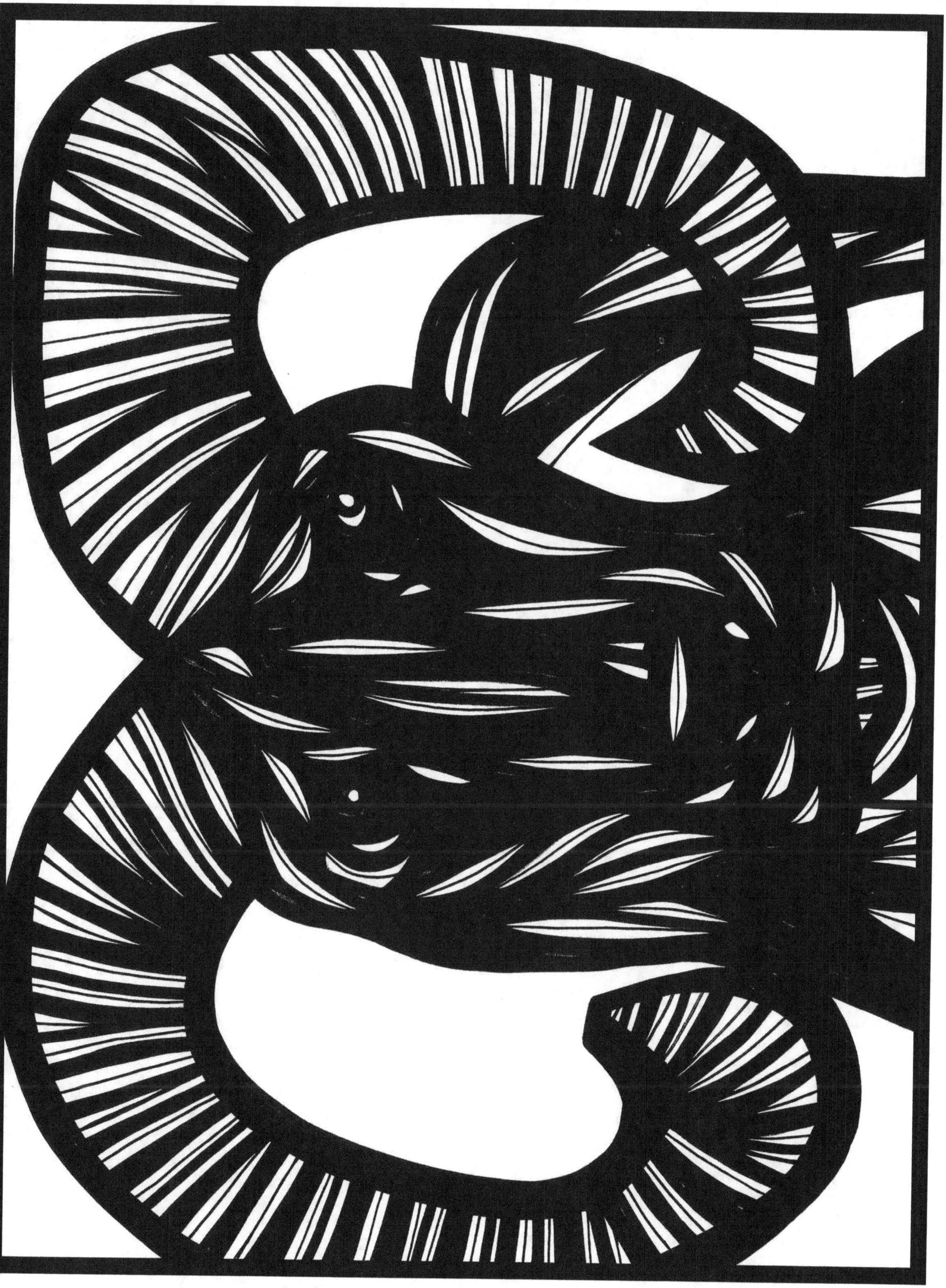

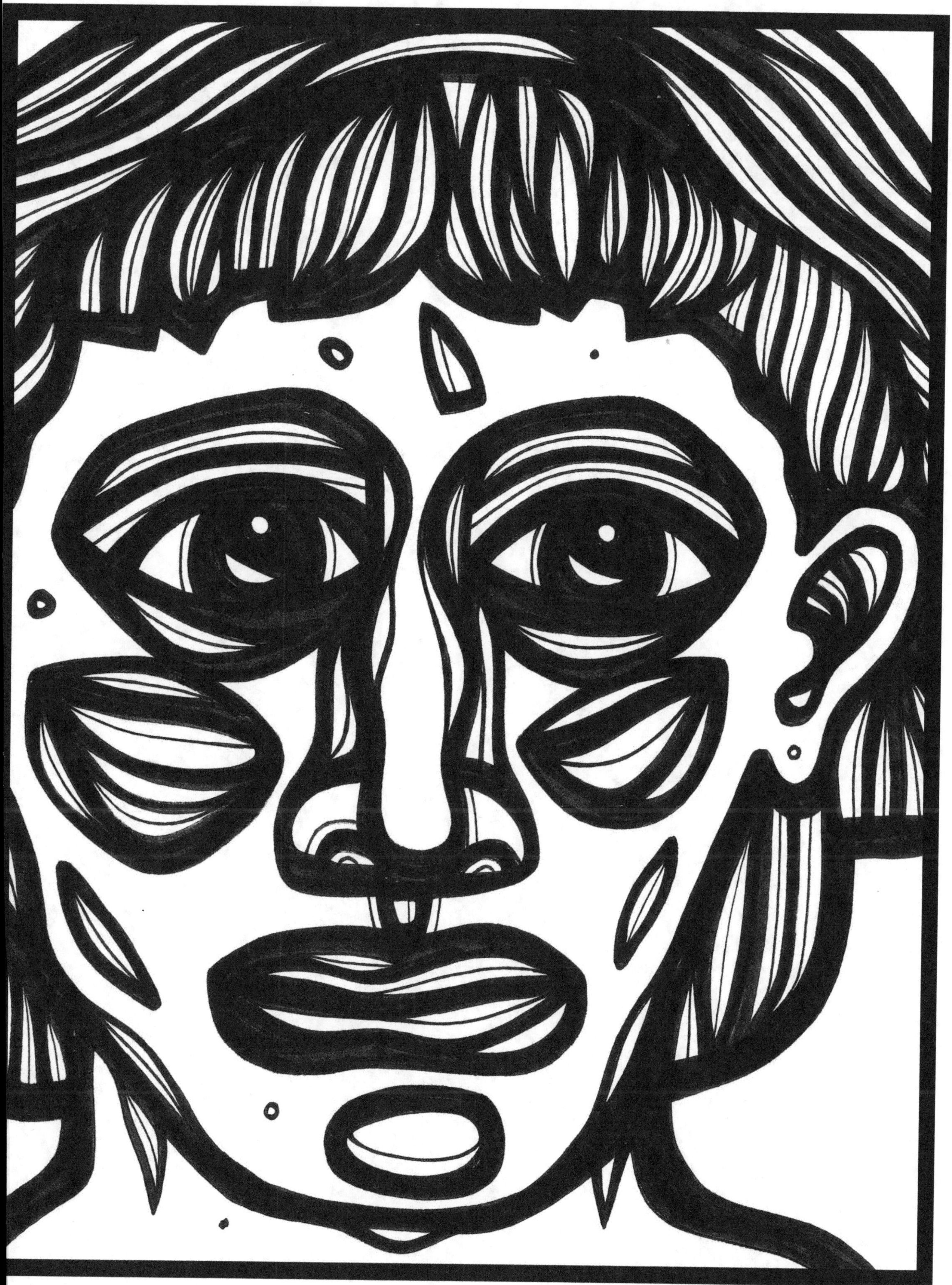

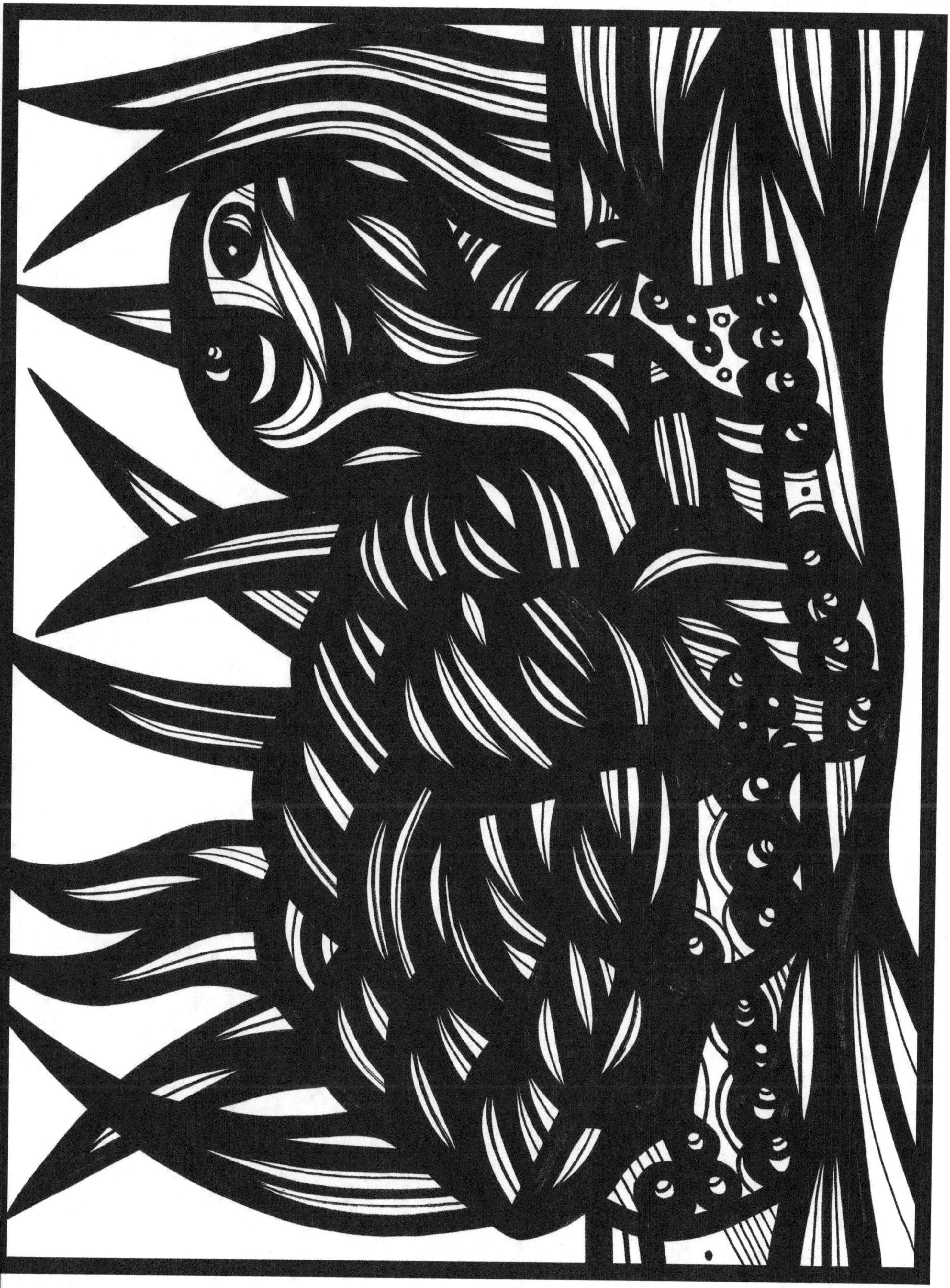

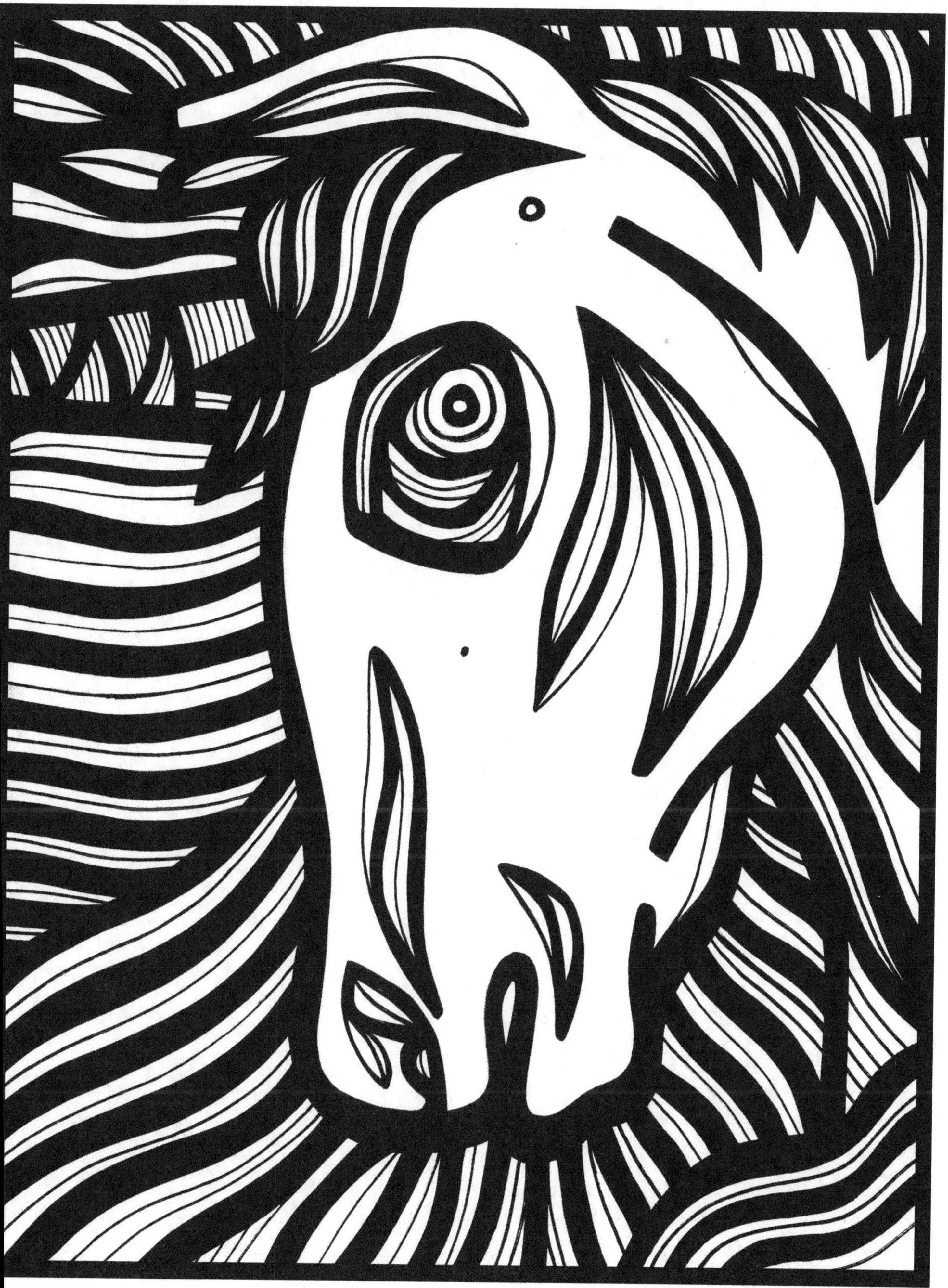

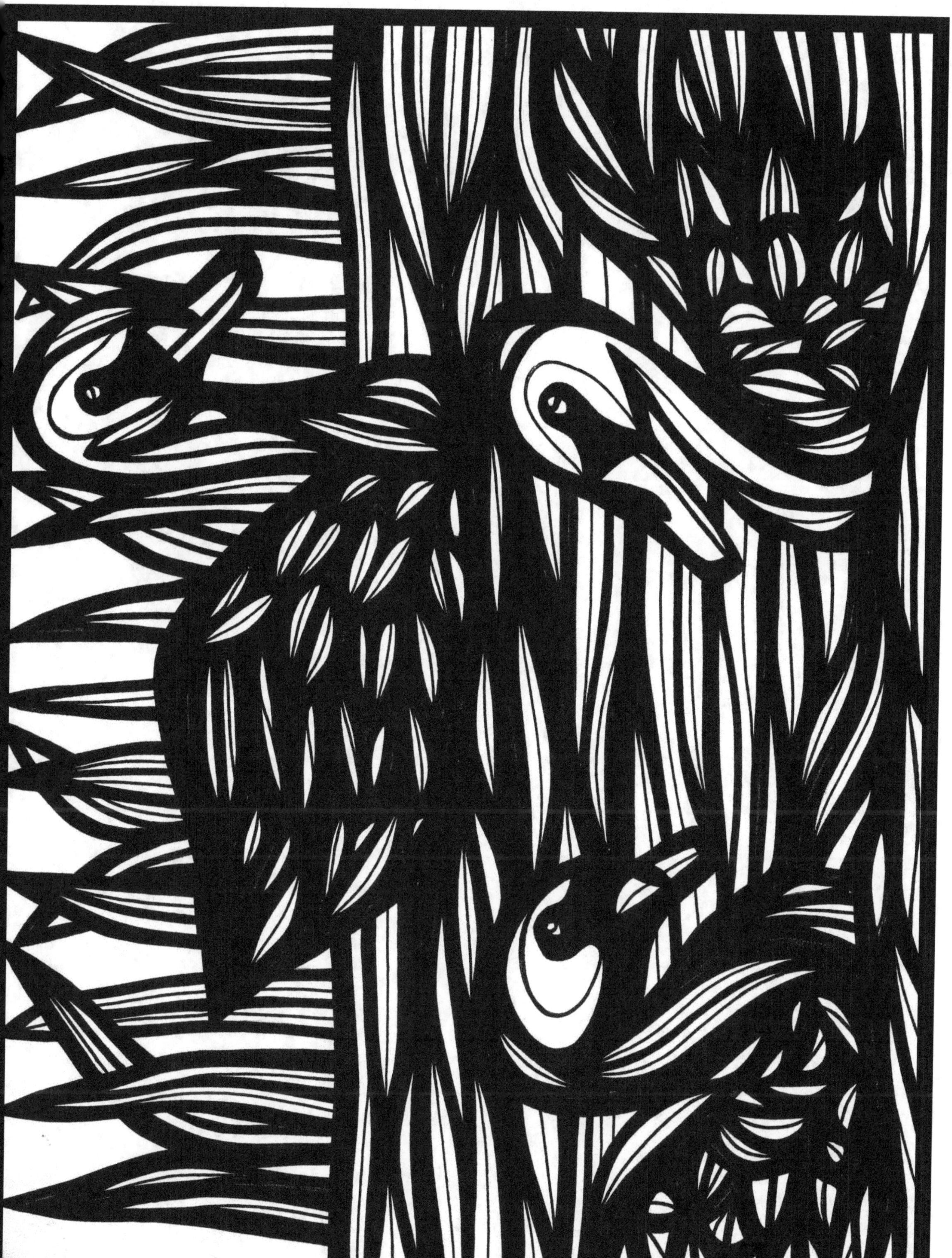

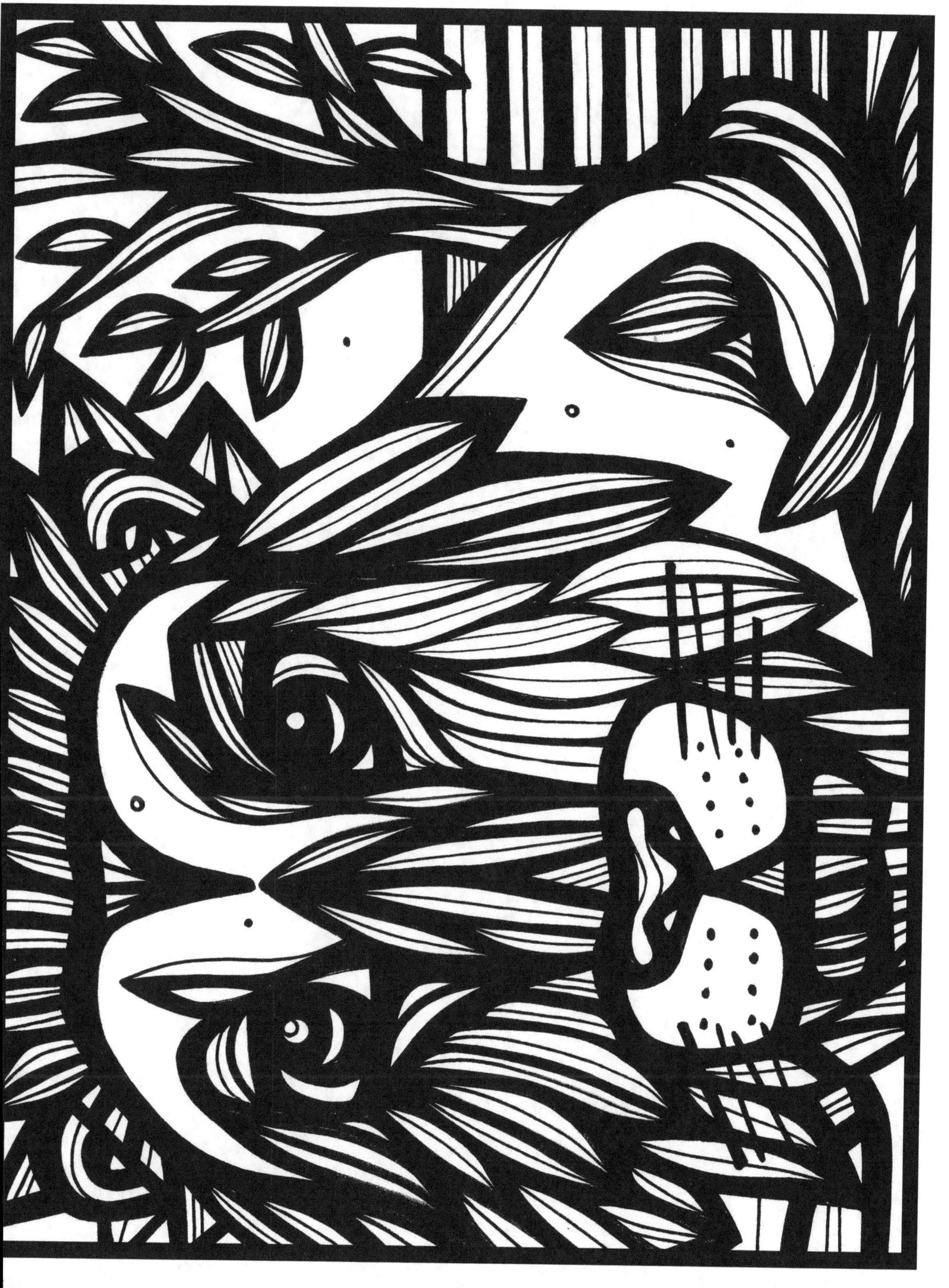

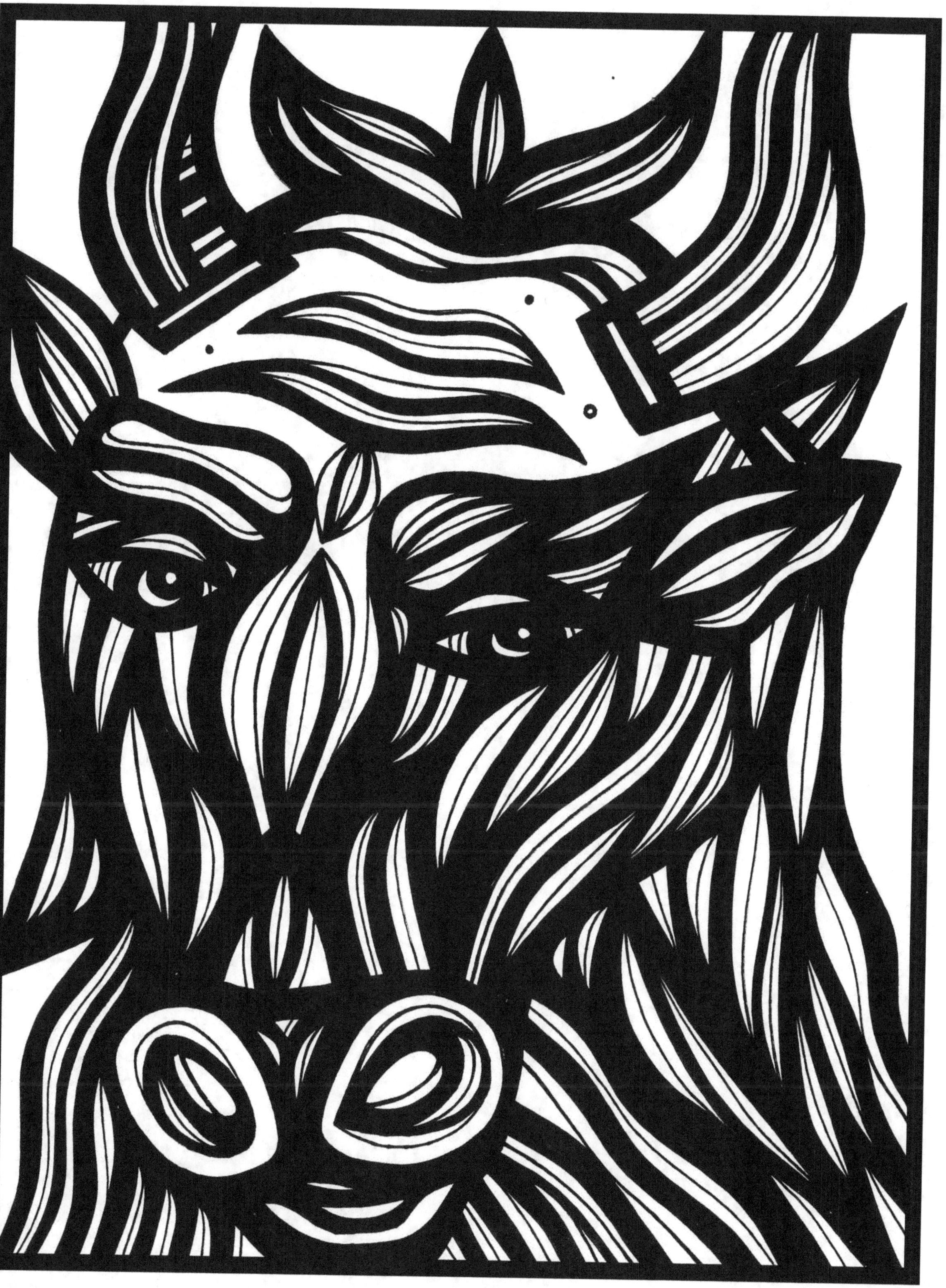

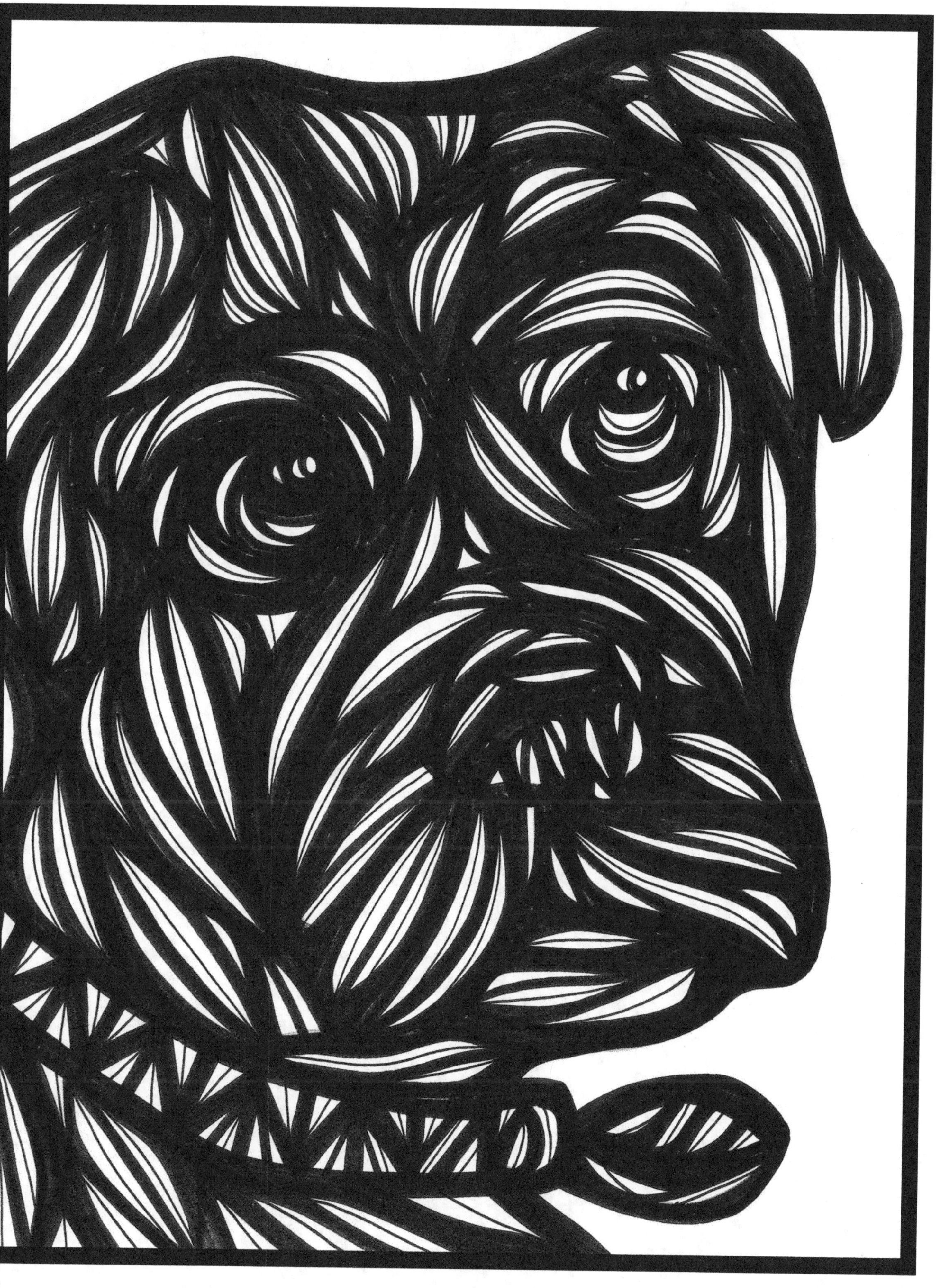

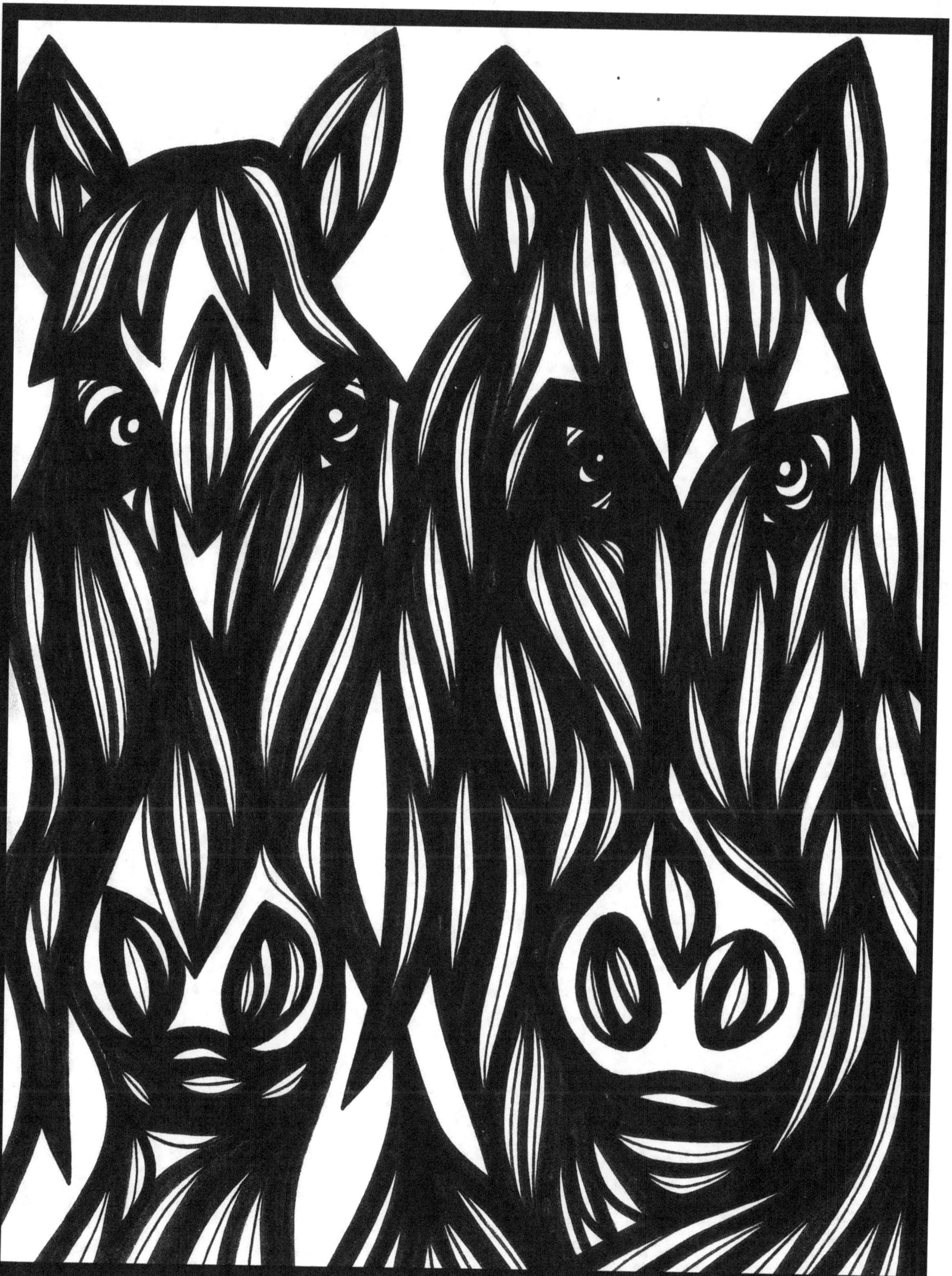

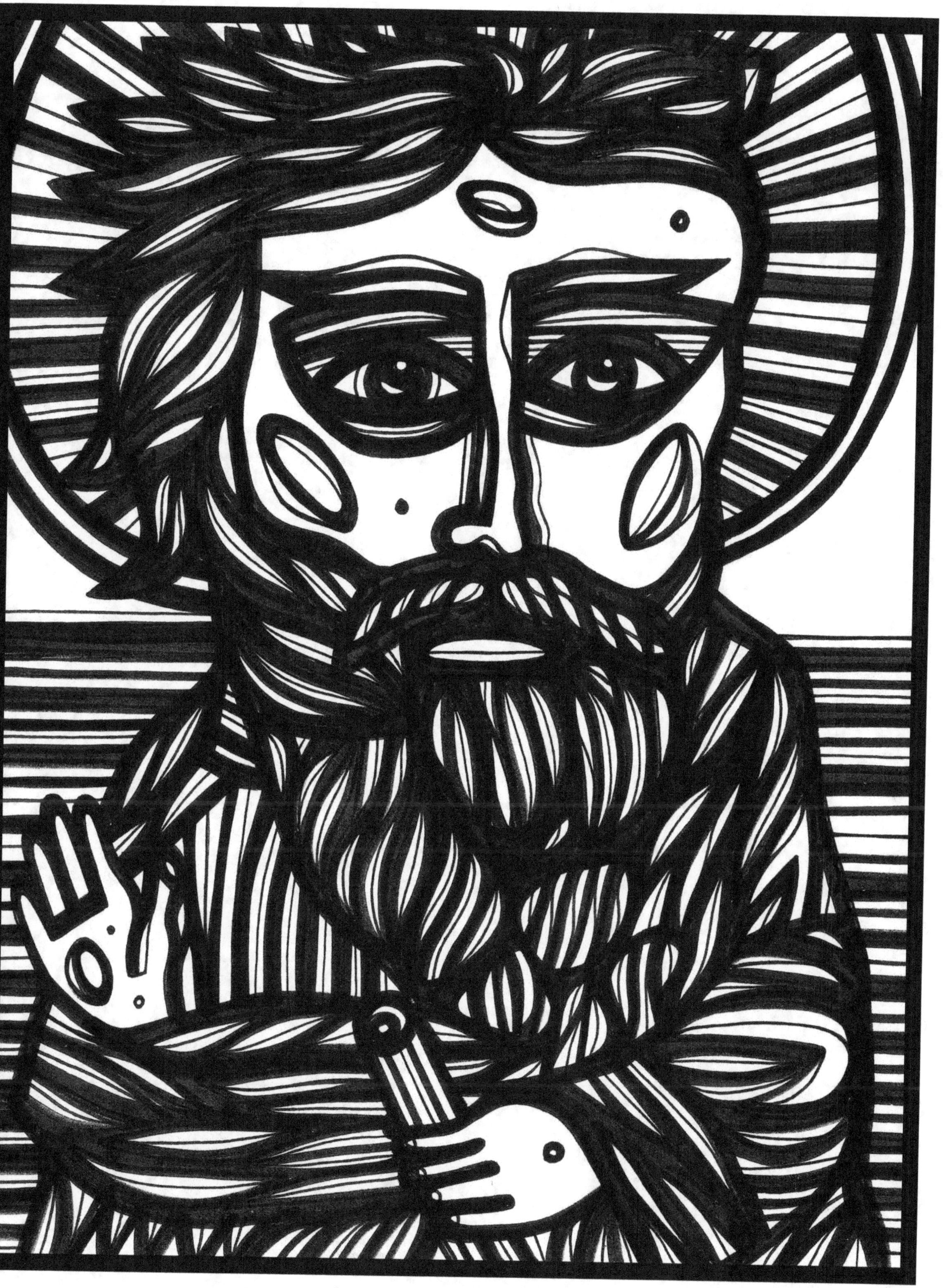

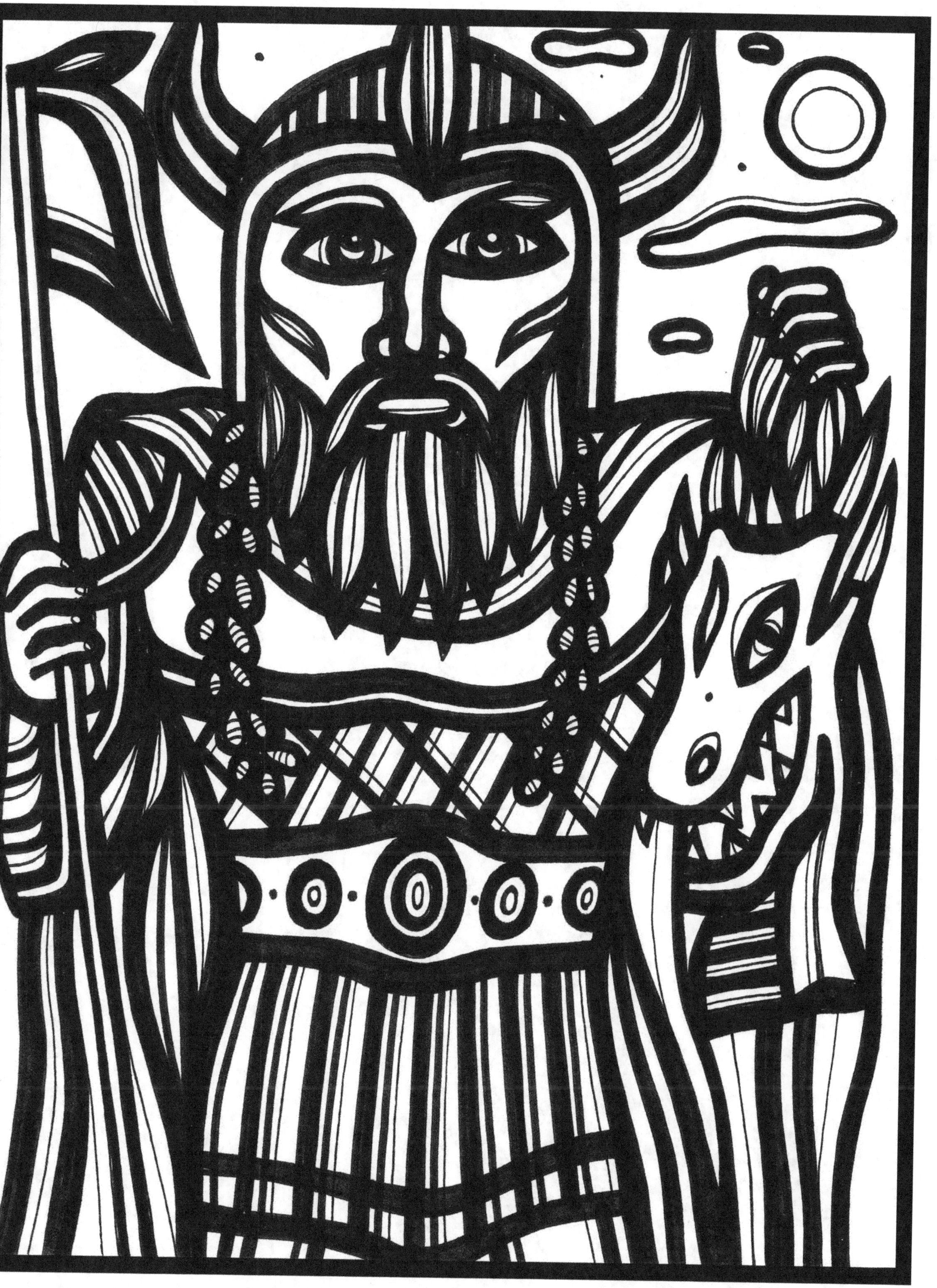

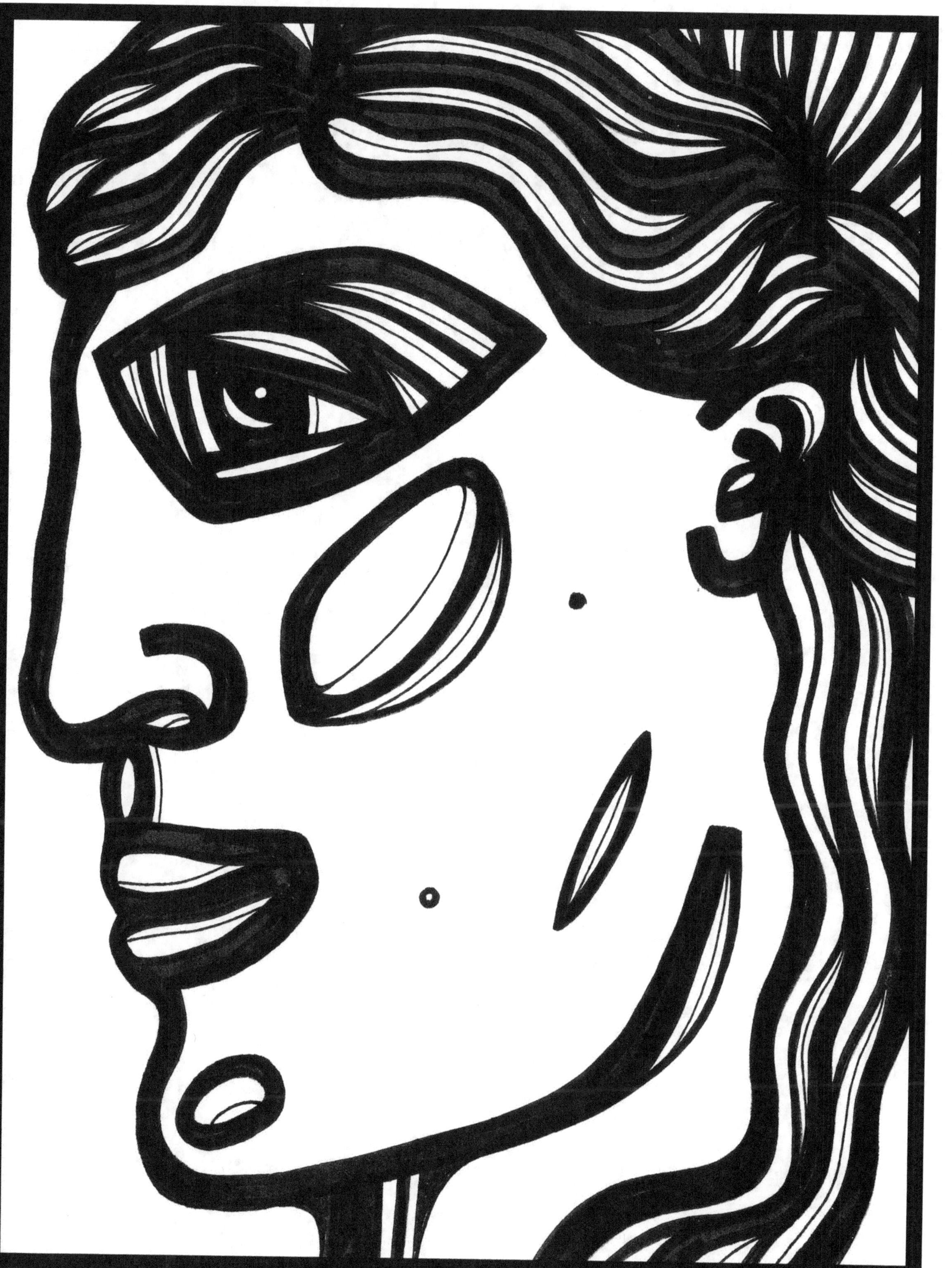

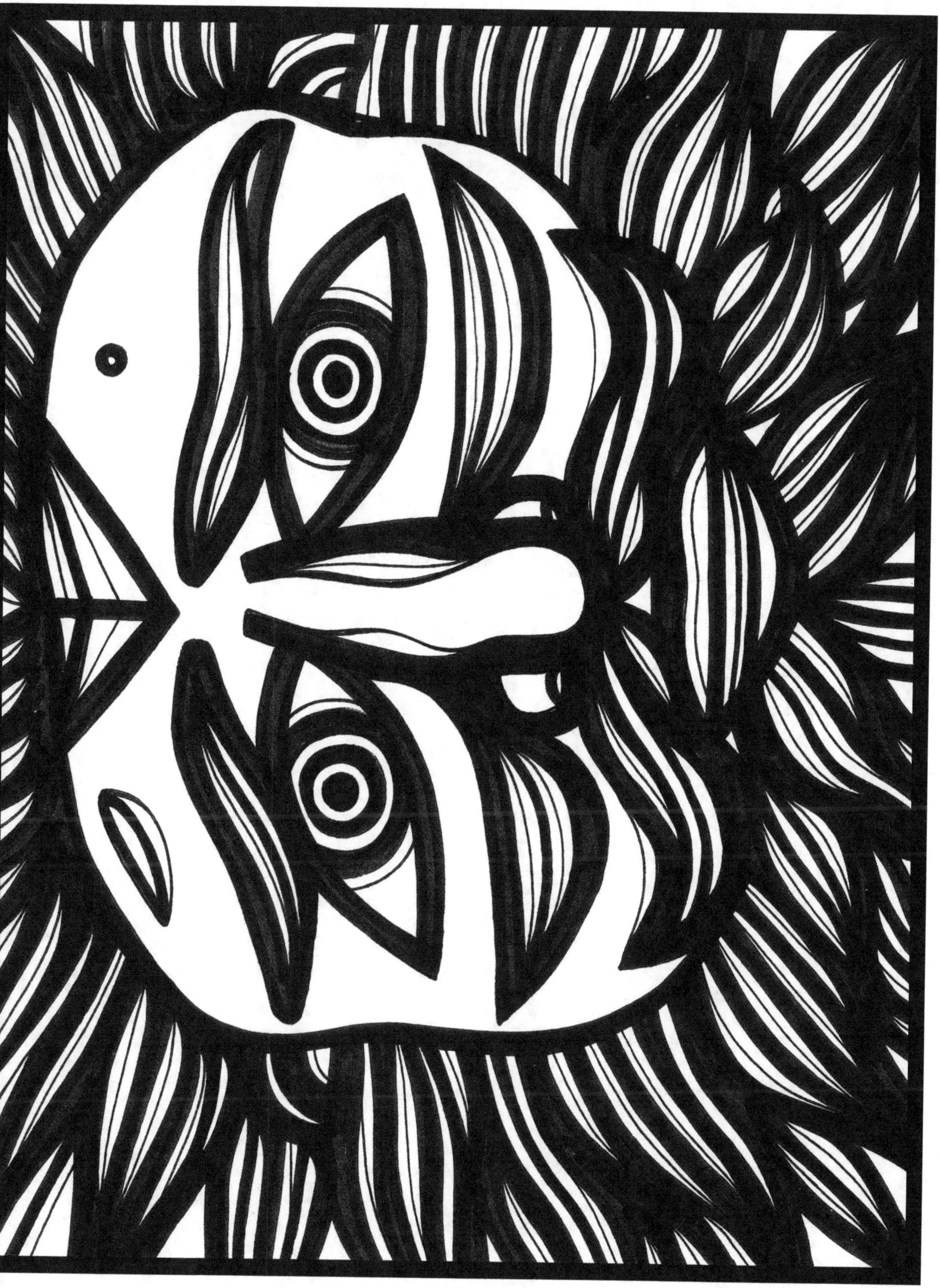

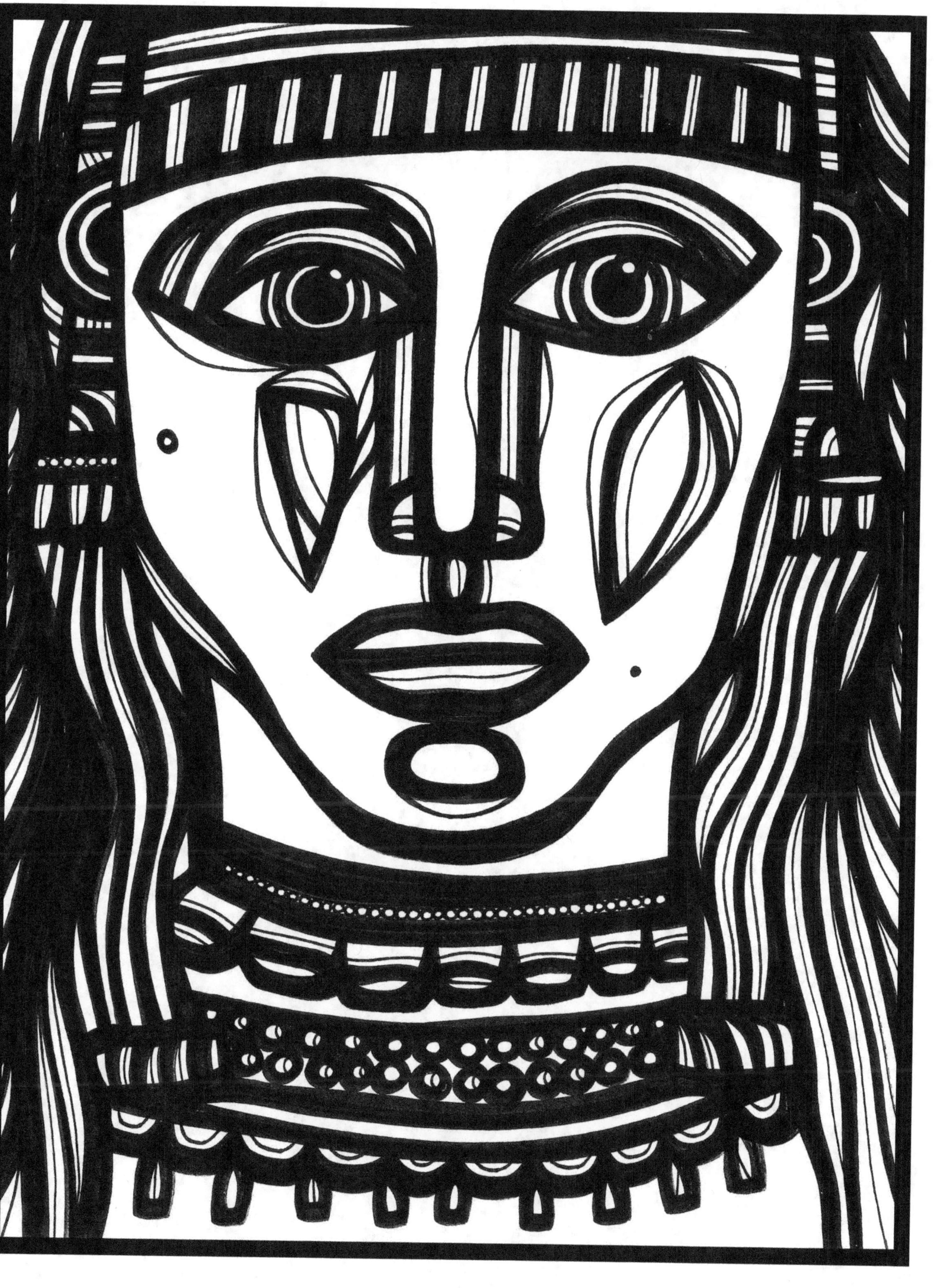

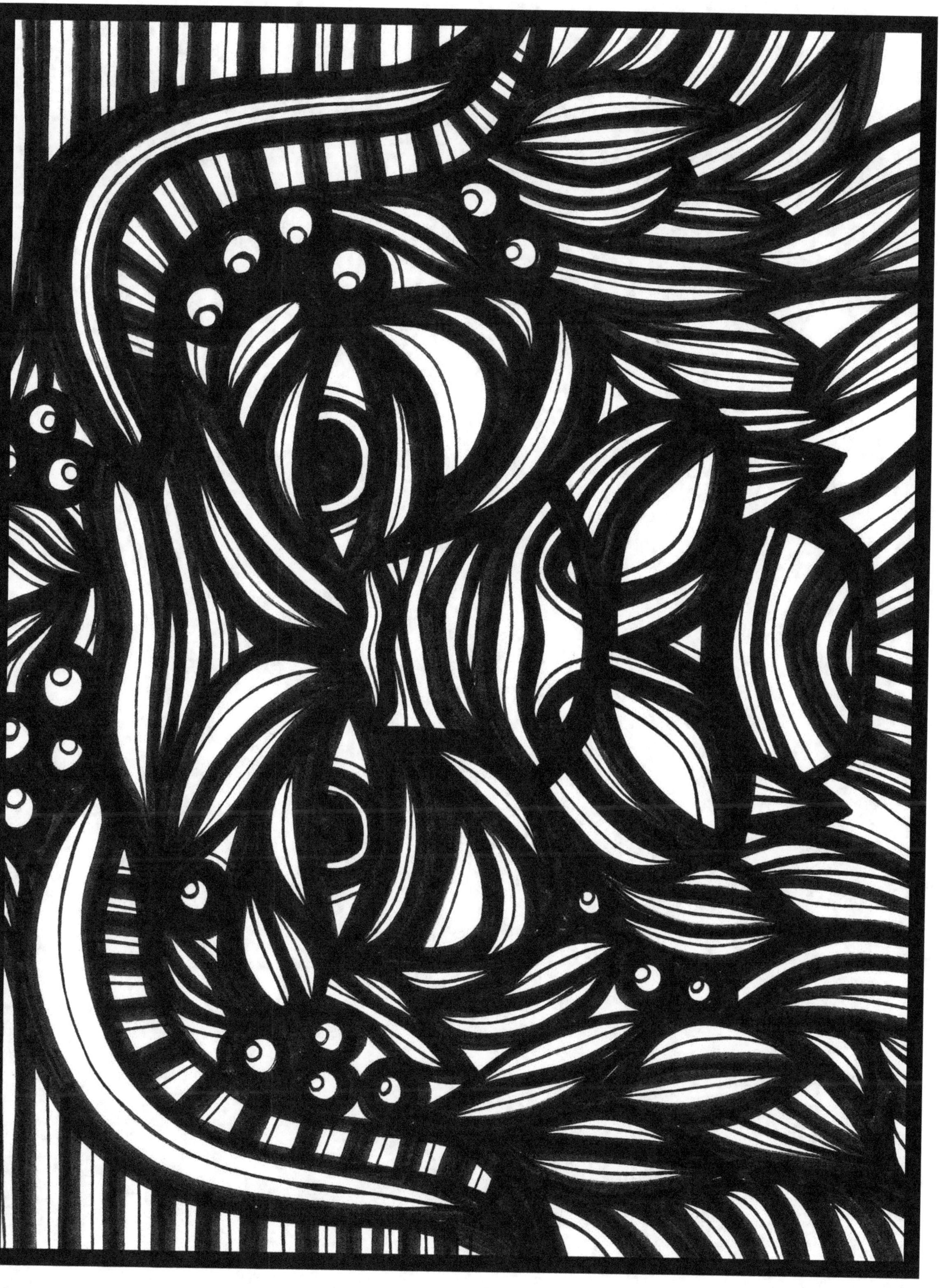

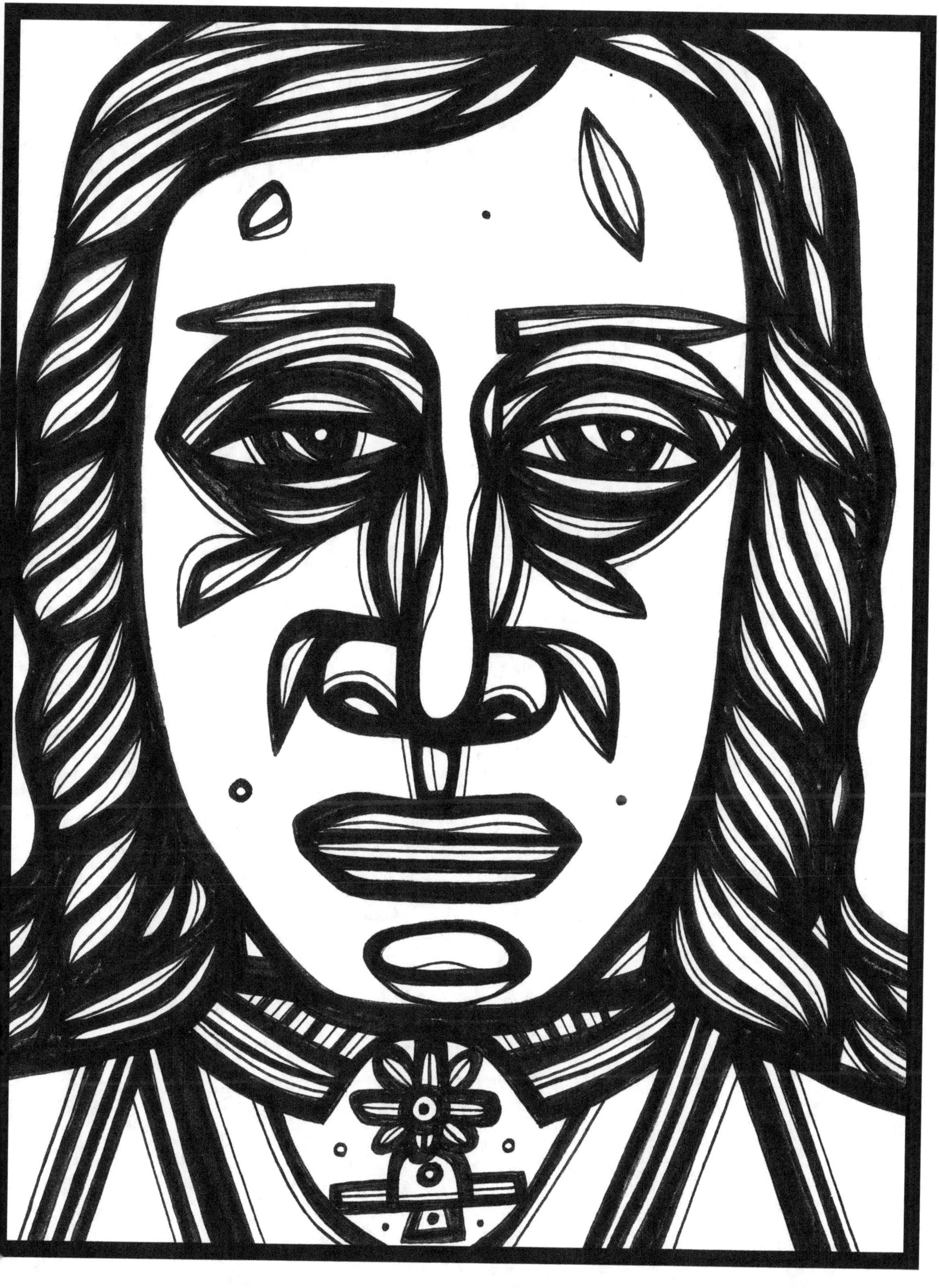

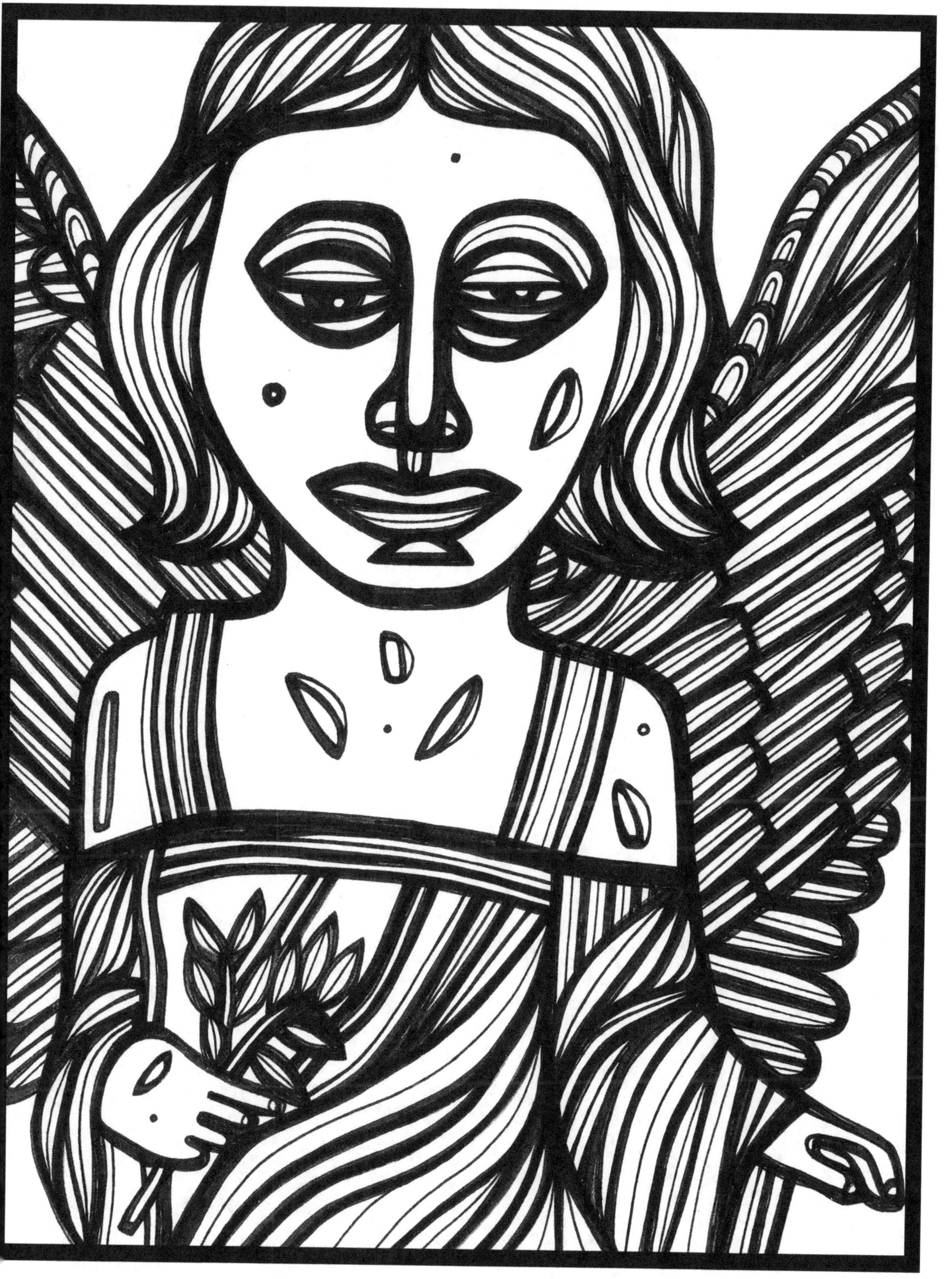

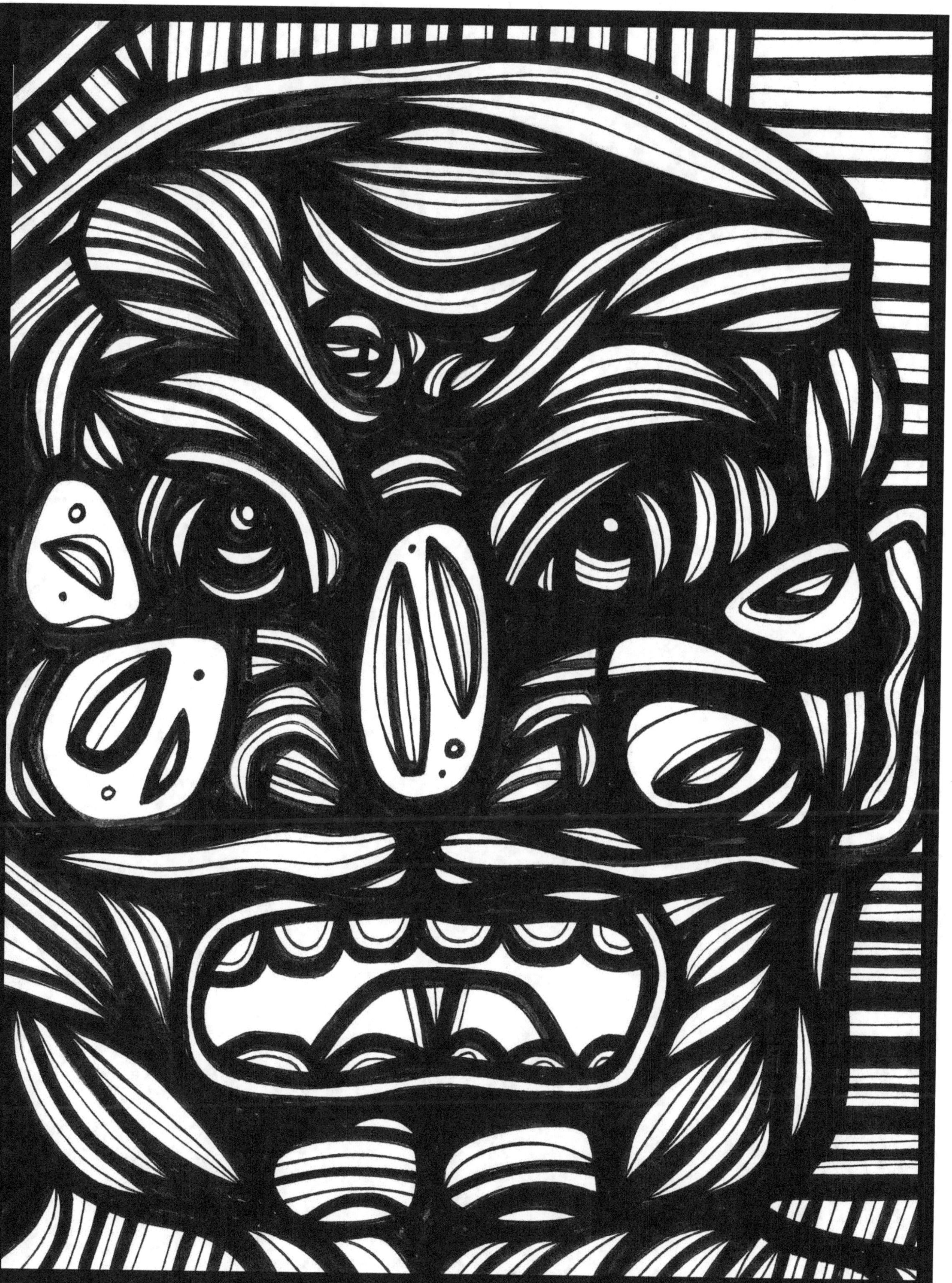

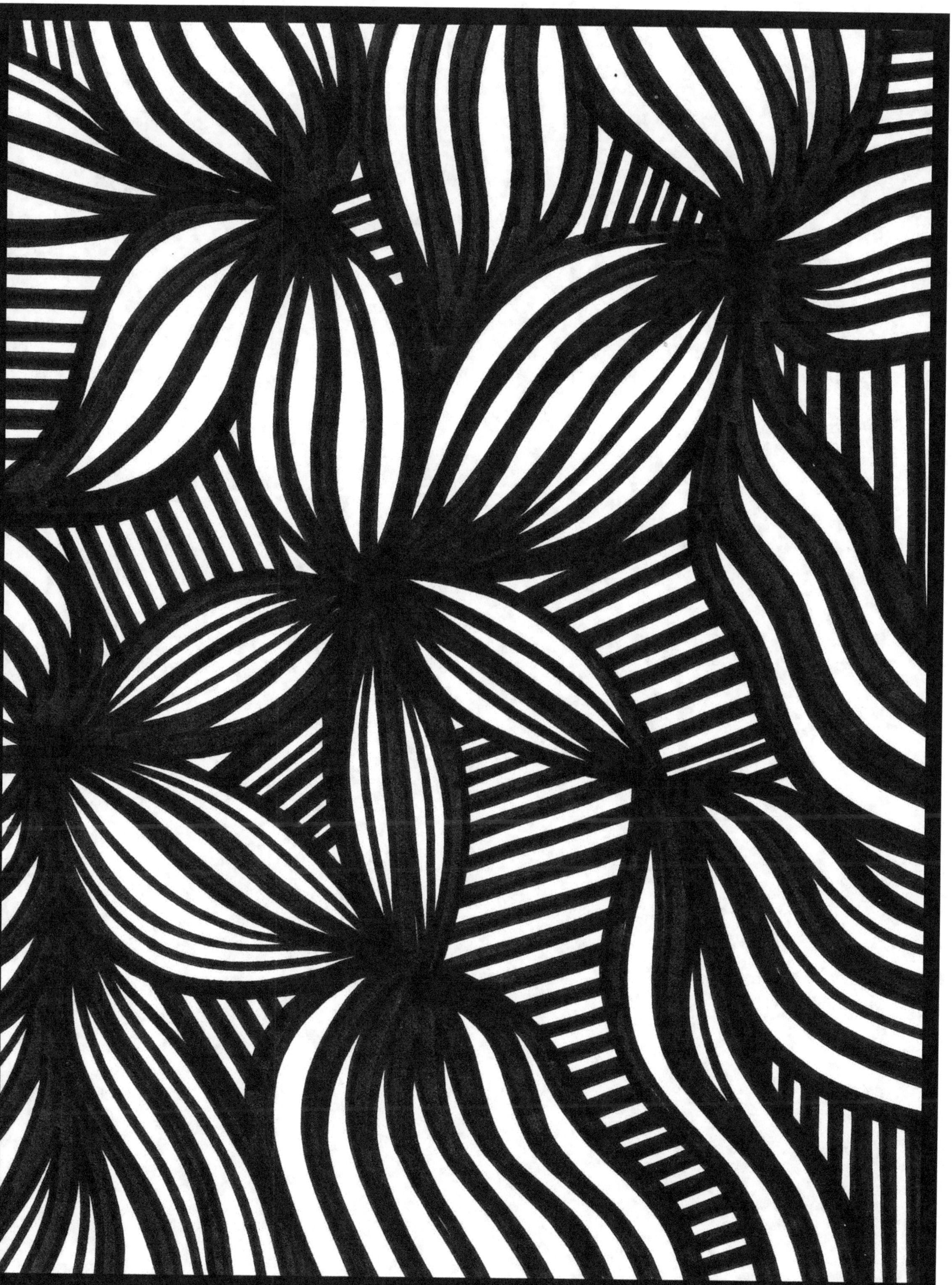

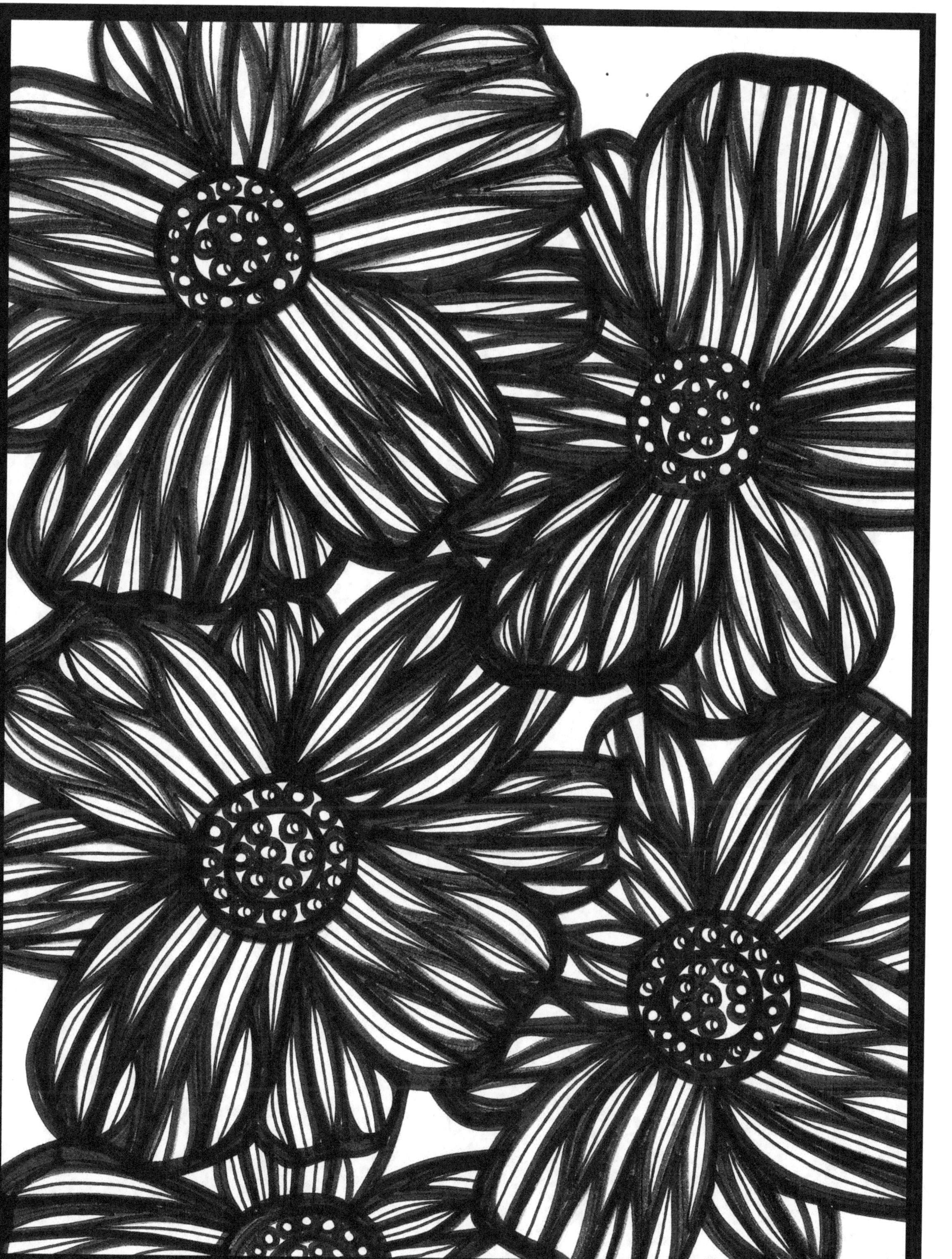

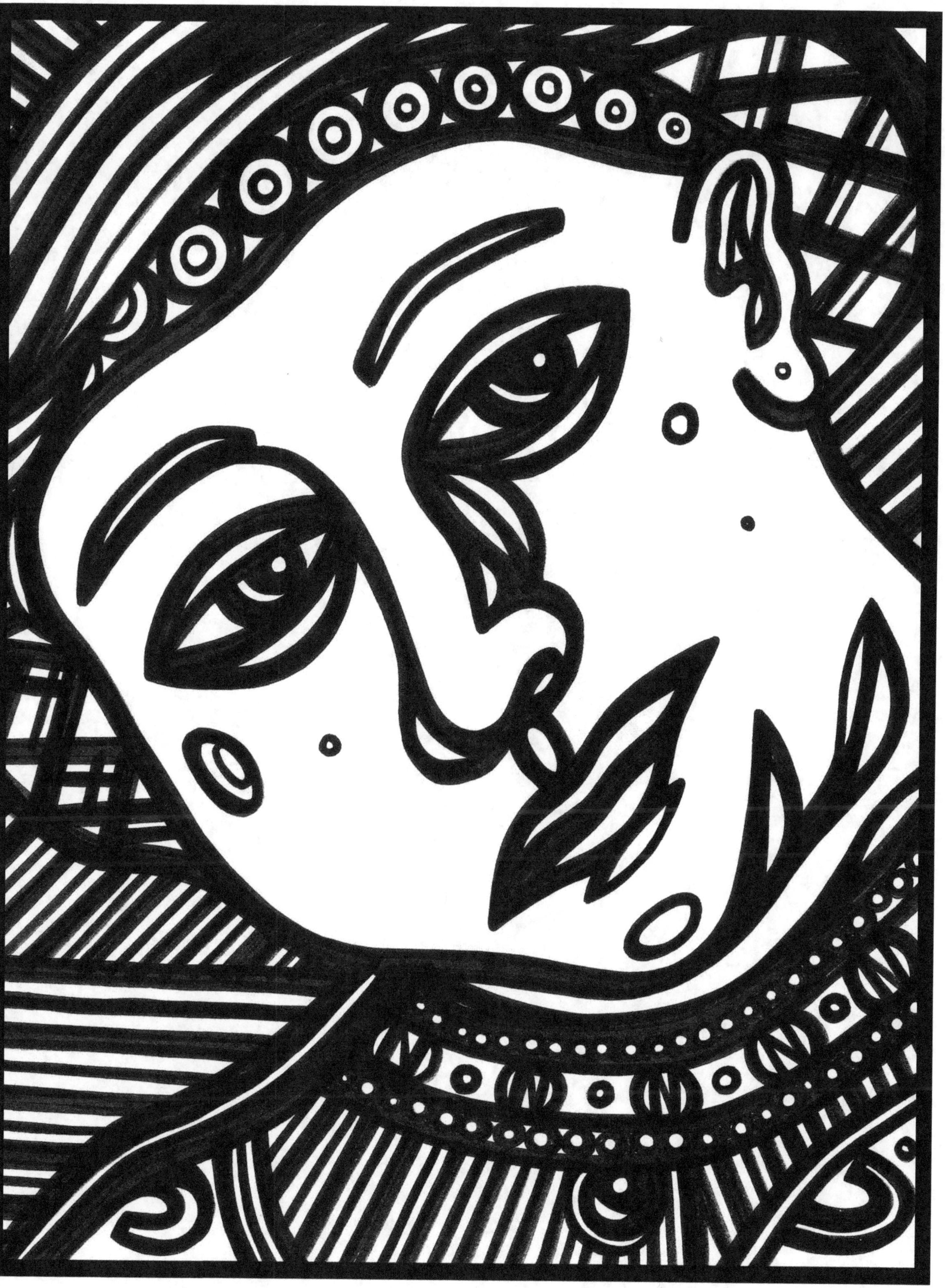

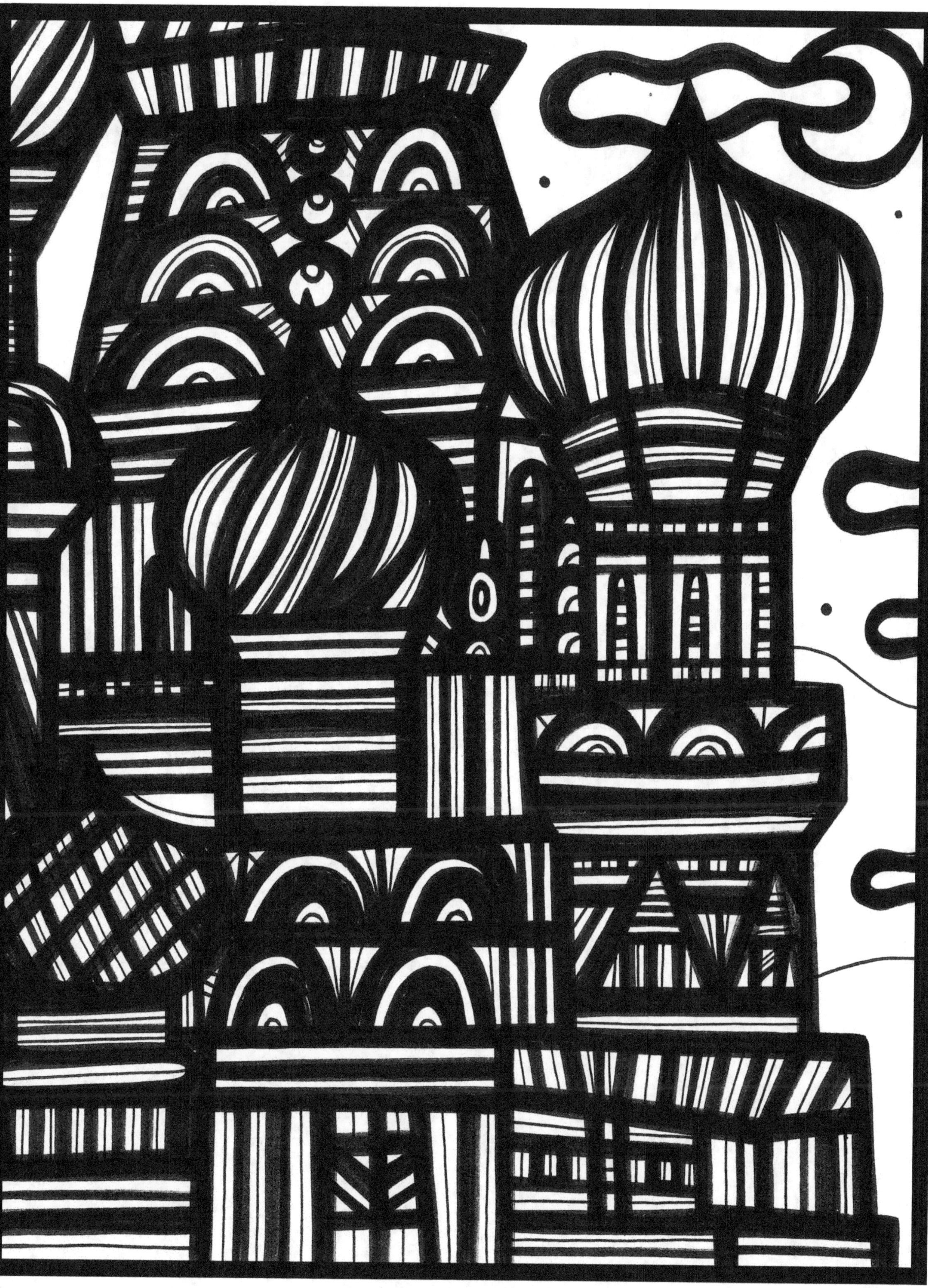

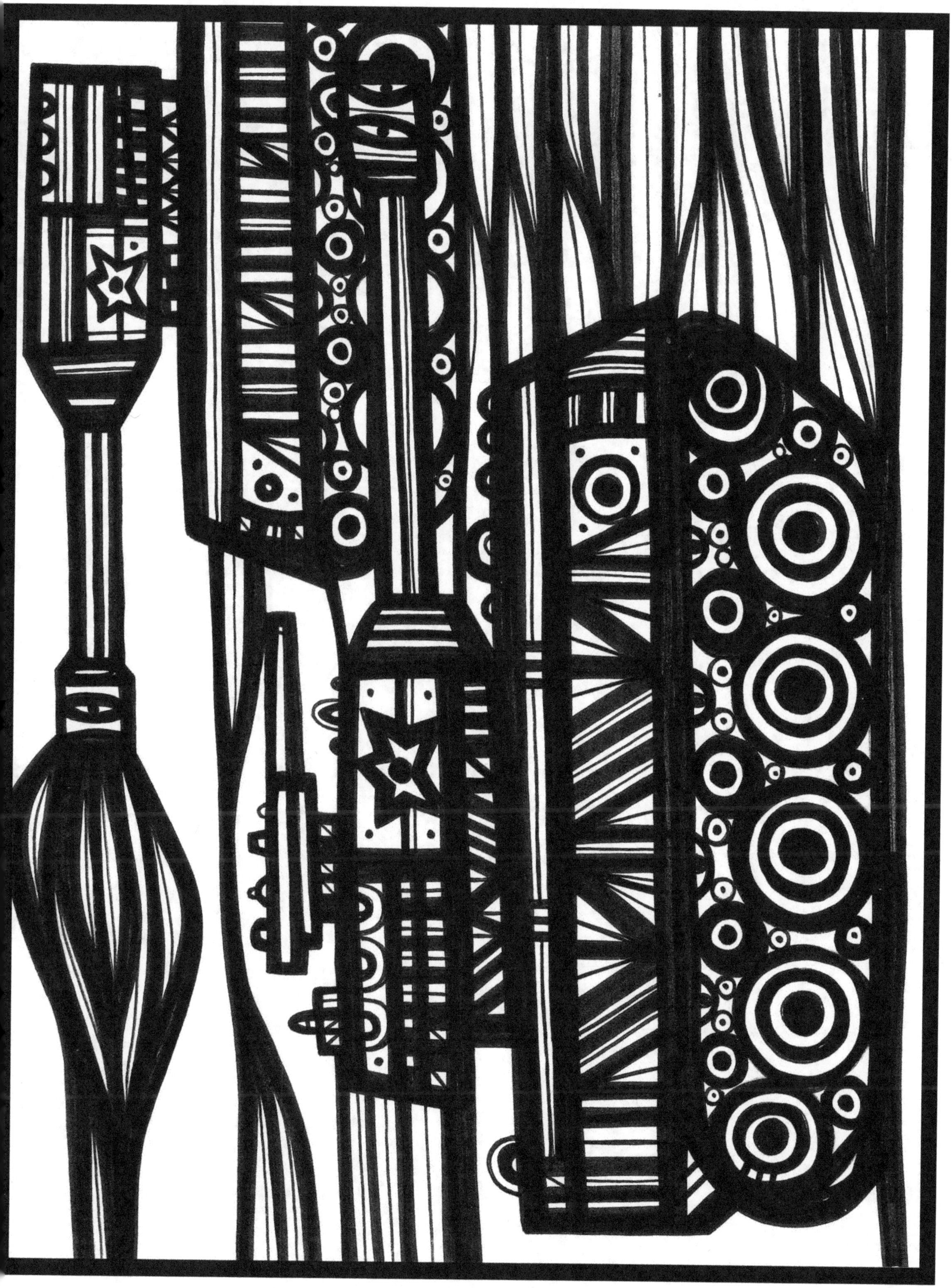

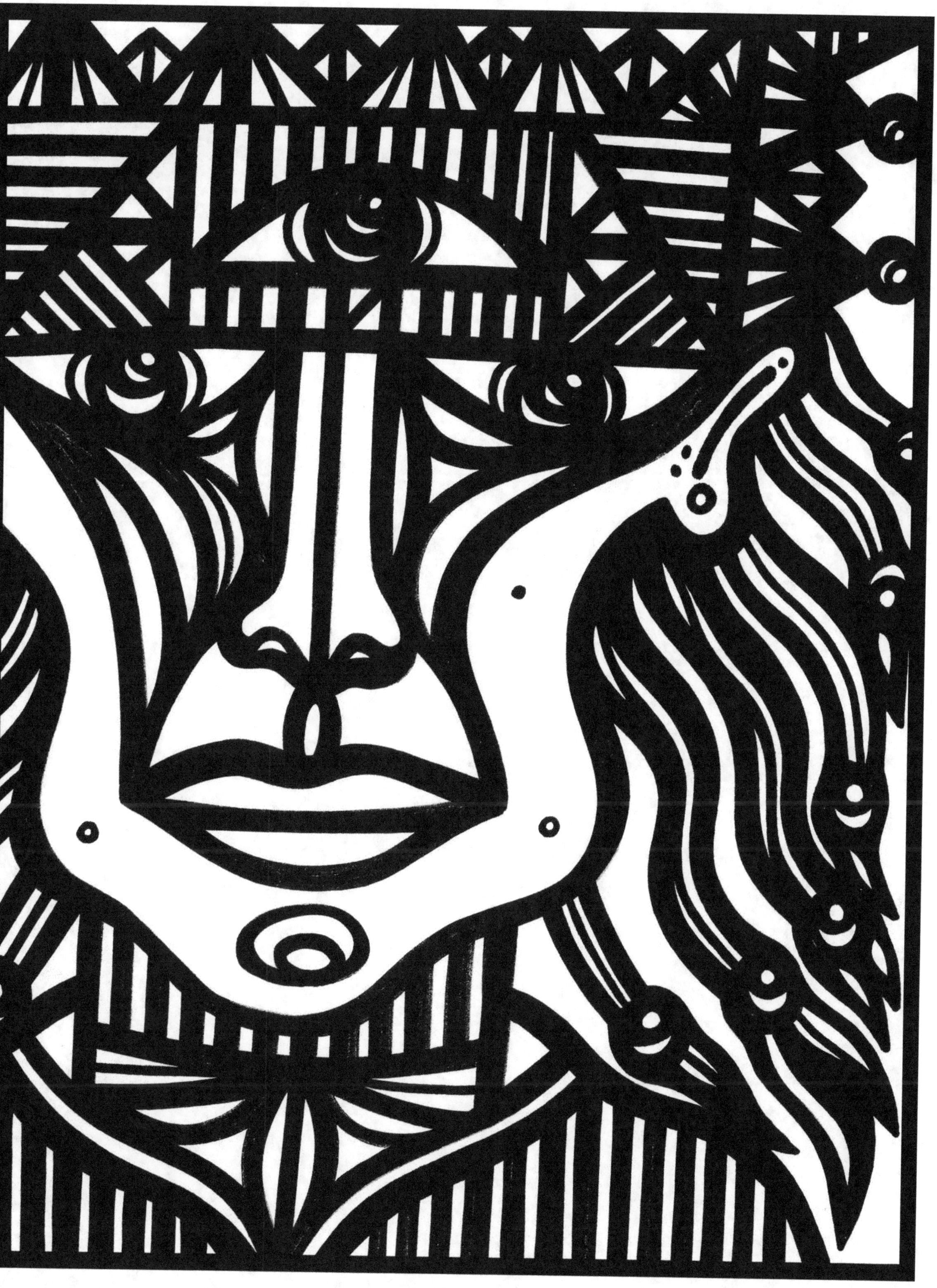

THE END,
THANK YOU!

MORE BOOKS:
631ART.COM

www.ingramcontent.com/pod-product-compliance
Lightning Source LLC
Chambersburg PA
CBHW080135240526
45468CB00009BA/2445
* 9 7 8 1 7 9 5 7 3 8 9 1 0 *